SUPERL

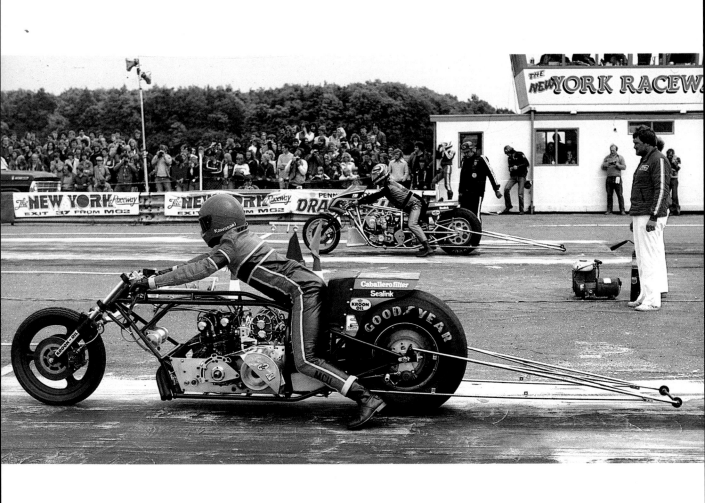

SUPERBIKES

Mick Woollett

B T Batsford Ltd, London

ISBN 0 7134 4172 0

Filmset by Servis Filmsetting Ltd, Manchester
and printed in Hong Kong
for the publishers
B T Batsford Ltd
4 Fitzhardinge Street
London W1H 0AH

Contents

Superbike of the 'thirties, the impressive 680cc vee-twin Brough Superior of 1932 complete with the now-back-in-fashion cantilever rear springing

Early Superbikes

The term Superbike was not coined until the late 'sixties when a catchword was needed to classify the new wave of large-capacity, high-performance machines. Yet Superbikes in one form or another have existed since the earliest years of the century.

Take a specification such as this: four cylinders in-line, water-cooling, shaft drive, full springing at front and rear and, for good measure, a luxurious car-type bucket seat. A Superbike by any standard . . . that was the Wilkinson TMC, made by the famous British sword and razor-blade company from 1912 until the overwhelming demand for cavalry swords for use in World War One curtailed production.

In fact Wilkinson's had made a shaft-drive four

An in-line, air-cooled, shaft-drive Wilkinson of 1911. A water-cooled version followed a year later but a huge contract for cavalry swords for World War One stopped production a couple of years later

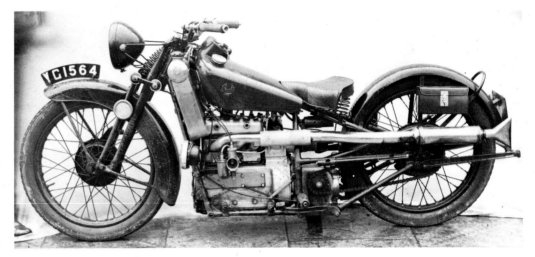

Nothing new under the sun . . . this 1934 water-cooled three-cylinder, two-stroke 750cc Scott was on the market some 40 years before the somewhat similar Suzuki. A 1000cc model was produced in 1936

from 1909 but the early models were air-cooled. And this, remember, at a time when the usual motor cycle was a single-cylinder side valve with non-detachable head, equipped with bicycle pedals to give assistance to the weak-kneed motor on anything worth calling a hill. Transmission would almost certainly have been by a stretchy (and in wet weather, slipping) vee-belt – and if there was any gearing at all, it would probably have been by an epicyclic rear hub, just a slightly more robust version of the cyclist's familiar Sturmey-Archer.

Even so, the Wilkinson was not the first shaft-drive four-in-line. That honour goes to the Belgian-based FN factory, the same concern that today supplies rifles to the NATO forces. Designed by Paul Kelecom, the FN four was first produced in 1905, originally single-geared but soon with a small two-speed gearbox incorporated in the drive-shaft train. Made in quite large quantities it was exported both to Britain and America and several examples have survived.

One American who fell in love with the FN four was Percy Pierce. Buying one while on a visit to Europe, he took it back to the States and there got his father's company, the Pierce Cycle Company of Buffalo, New York, to design a bike that owed its general layout to the FN but was otherwise

decidedly a Superbike, even carrying fuel and oil in its large-diameter frame tubes.

Launched in 1909, the Pierce started a trend in the USA and, in time, a whole flock of other in-line fours came along: Henderson, Cleveland, Ace and eventually the Indian Four which was produced right into the early 1940s. However, the American motor cycle makers had to contend with the cheap mass-produced cars and it was not until recent years that motor cycling acquired much of a hold in that vast continent.

It was a different story in Europe and, especially, Britain where for a couple of decades the motor cycle was for many people essential daily transport. For that reason it had to be kept simple, reliable and, above all, cheap. Yet for all the prudence and frugality there was still room at the very top of the market for a few exclusive machines, made with the very best of available materials for those who could afford such a necessarily high-priced model.

High priest of Superbike makers was Nottingham's George Brough. Indeed, he even named his marque the Brough Superior and advertised it (presumably with permission) as 'The Rolls Royce of Motor Cycles'. George did not make his own power units but instead opted for engines built by J A Prestwich of Tottenham,

Motosacoche of Switzerland and Matchless of Woolwich. Not your common-or-garden JAP, MAG or Matchless but ones made to his own exacting requirements.

Frankly, much of this was ballyhoo but the fact remains that the Brough Superior became the status symbol of its time and could number among its owners as illustrious a personage as Lawrence of Arabia.

From time to time George would produce, usually as a surprise for the London Show, an even more superior Brough Superior. Usually it was a four – a straight air-cooled four, a transverse vee-four, a water-cooled Austin-engined four (but not powered by a standard Austin Seven power unit. It was, as George pointed out,

Probably the best American big bike of the 'thirties, the imposing Indian Four of 1935, derived from the earlier Ace Four

One of the famous
Superbikes of the pre-war
era, the Ariel Square
Four. This is the 1938
version with 1000cc engine

Opposite Modern-day
picture of the bike that
started the Superbike
trend, the four-cylinder,
shaft drive Belgian FN

a special 800cc version, built for him by his
personal friend Lord Austin).

Last of the line was Brough's Superbike of
Superbikes, a transverse flat-four with shaft drive
and, as a special Earls Court Show attraction, a
metallic gold colour scheme. Alas, World War
Two arrived before the Golden Dream reached
production and now just two prototypes remain
as a hint of what might have been.

Although George Brough was undoubtedly
the most flamboyant of the Superbike makers of
the 'twenties and 'thirties he was certainly not the
only one. From way down in Exeter, Jack
Wheaton evolved the highly sophisticated AJW

Super 4 with a car-type pressed-steel chassis in
which sat a water-cooled Anzani four engine. It
stole the headlines, then disappeared to emerge in
sidecar racing trim – unsuccessfully, it trans-
pired. Even Vauxhall, the car manufacturers,
thought about venturing on to two wheels with a
very advanced machine (a straight four) but
abandoned the idea after building a couple of
prototypes – one of which survives in an Isle of
Man motor museum.

The true vintage era is generally considered to
have ended in 1930, the year in which the effect of
the Wall Street crash was beginning to be felt all
around the world. Certainly there were hard

times ahead but perversely, the 1930 London Show saw the introduction of a British-made Superbike that was to prove a lasting success.

This was Edward Turner's immortal Ariel Square Four, so named because the cylinders were arranged two by two (really two vertical twins, set one behind the other and geared together). At first a 500cc, the Square Four grew to 600cc then at last to a massive 1000cc. 'Ten to a hundred in top gear', claimed the makers – and they proved it in a test at the Brooklands racing circuit, home of British racing in the 'thirties.

At first, however, the Ariel did not have things all its own way. The same 1930 London Show saw the debut of another contender for status symbolism, this time from Matchless. It was the overhead-camshaft Silver Hawk and although the engine looked like a square four it was actually a narrow-angle vee-four.

Beautifully made, beautifully smooth in its power delivery, it had one potential plus over the Ariel in the form of cantilever rear springing. But in the depressed trading conditions of the time there was only room at the top of the heap for one machine and, after fighting a losing battle, the Matchless faded from the scene.

Even the deepest depression must end some time and as the sad 'thirties rolled on so the skies did begin to brighten just a little. There were even a few more luxury bikes with exotic specifications to come – though the three-cylinder, water-cooled, two-stroke Scott of 1937 was made in only extremely limited numbers. A more lasting design came from Stevenage, the first 1000cc vee-twin Vincent-HRD.

Most exotic of them all was proposed by AJS – an overhead camshaft vee-four with provision for supercharging. In time to come, that model would be developed for grand prix racing, not only supercharged but with liquid cooling. The final works-racer version can be seen in Sammy Miller's museum at New Milton. But the original AJS plan was to market it as a sports roadster. If only they had gone ahead on those lines: what a Superbike that would have been!

The Untapped Market

Typical of the British models developed for the American market – the 650cc AJS vertical twin of 1959

Although Superbikes of one sort or another have been built in limited numbers since the turn of the century the market for large-capacity, high-performance, glamour machines remained untapped and unprovided for until the end of the 'sixties.

It was then that both the British and Japanese manufacturers realised that there was a market for motor cycles that were in many ways illogical. That were brutishly powerful, extremely fast and above all strikingly good to look at.

The demand came first from America where a new section of society, the young on near adult wages and with surplus cash, had developed and were seeking status symbols on which to spend this new wealth. This available cash coincided with the rise of Japanese industry – and with the struggle of the British and other European manufacturers to keep one jump ahead of the thrusting oriental challengers.

Norton's answer to the demand for high performance machines – the 650SS of 1966

The Japanese had entered the world market in the early 'sixties with lightweight machines and had gradually expanded up the capacity scale. The massive advertising campaigns they mounted in the fickle American market had created a demand not just for their light and middle-range machines but also for the bigger bikes made by the American Harley Davidson factory and by the European makers led by BSA, Triumph, Norton and BMW.

Harley Davidson had always built big machines but these were extremely heavy and were powered by large but relatively inefficient engines and, while they had their devotees, they were not what the new wave of motor cyclists wanted.

To cater for the American taste for bigger machines BSA, Triumph, Ariel, Royal Enfield, Matchless, AJS and Norton had during the 'fifties produced 650cc or 600cc versions of their existing 500cc models while Ariel continued to produce one of the original Superbikes – the famous 1000cc Square Four. However, if truth be told, the Square Four engine was never very powerful and tended to overheat if ridden hard because the rear pair of cylinders were masked from the cooling air-flow by the front pair.

BMW, too, had 600cc models in their range but

ironically the first true Superbike, although the name was not coined until after its demise, was the British Vincent 998cc vee-twin. Superbly designed it combined truly high performance with stylish good looks that are modern and eye-catching to this day.

The top model of the Vincent range of sports roadsters was the Black Shadow. Powered by a 55hp version of the big-twin engine, it weighed only 458lb fully equipped for the road and had a top speed of close to 120mph, which, in those days, made the Vincent far and away the fastest bike you could buy for road use. If you wanted a quicker one you could always purchase the racing version, the stripped for action and more highly tuned Black Lightning competition model. On one of these the American, Rowland Free had set numerous records at Bonneville in 1950 including covering ten miles at just over 154mph, and that without any form of streamlining at all!

Unfortunately though, Vincent were in the market before the demand for Superbikes was more than just a trickle and in the mid-'fifties they went out of business. If only they could have hung on until the motor cycle boom of the 'sixties. . . .

BSA/Triumph, who had amalgamated in an

Trend-setting Superbike – the 998cc Vincent Black Shadow vee-twin of the early 'fifties

British Superbike – the 1969 three-cylinder BSA Rocket 3 750cc sports roadster

attempt to fight the Japanese challenge, and Honda, both realised the potential of the Super-bike market at about the same time and both started to design and develop sophisticated multi-cylinder 750cc machines in the mid-'sixties.

Honda won the race to the market place. They officially launched their CB750 at the Tokyo Show in October 1968 and the machine was in volume-production the next year.

Clearly influenced by their racing machines the original CB750 was powered by a beautifully engineered air-cooled, four-cylinder, four-stroke engine with single overhead camshaft valve operation and a five-speed gearbox. Power output was around the 75bhp mark with the engine red-lined at 8500.

Launched over 20 years ago but still a stylish sports machine – the 1968 650cc B.S.A Spitfire

The Italians were first with a six-cylinder Superbike. This is the Benelli prototype 750cc straight six of the mid 'seventies.

Black and gold – 1971 750cc vertical twin Norton Commando on show

Top speed was 120mph and although the handling left something to be desired, the CB750 proved a best seller and over one million of this and subsequent CB750 models were sold during the following decade.

Sadly, as far as the British industry was concerned the BSA/Triumph and Norton models could not compete. The BSA/Triumph was a three-cylinder, push-rod 750cc which went extremely well in racing trim, scoring an impressive 1-2-3 in the Daytona 200 in 1971 but was nothing like so reliable or trouble free as the Honda in standard form and which, in the States, actually cost more than the Honda.

Norton countered by introducing the 750cc Commando, mounting the massive vertical twin-cylinder engine in rubber to damp out the vibration inherent in this design. It succeeded to a limited degree but within a few years both of the British concerns had gone out of business leaving

Powerful Ducati – works 750cc sports racer of 1972. Engine is a vee-twin

the market to the Japanese; to BMW of Germany and to a handful of Italian makers headed by Ducati, Benelli and Moto Guzzi.

There is no doubt that Honda were surprised by the demand for the CB750 – not just from America where it was launched in Las Vegas at a dealer convention in January 1969, but from around the world. They, and all the other makers of large-capacity motor cycles, quickly realised that they had moved up into a new and, until the CB750 was launched, virtually untapped market.

Inevitably other manufacturers produced rival Superbikes – notably the 900cc Kawasaki launched in 1971, the first of a long line of four-cylinder, double overhead camshaft sports road-sters from Kawasaki; the 750cc three-cylinder, water-cooled Suzuki; the 1000cc range of BMW twins launched in 1976; the 750cc six-cylinder

The author tries the Honda CB750 at Brands Hatch early in 1969. This was the first time the bike that really started the Superbike trend had been ridden in England

*Suzuki's first Superbike –
the 750cc three-cylinder
water-cooled two-stroke of
the early 'seventies*

Benelli; the 900cc Ducati vee-twins; the 850cc Moto Guzzi and more recently the four-cylinder ranges developed by both Yamaha and Suzuki to counter the initial success of the Honda and Kawasaki models of this type.

So the scene was set for the Superbike sales battle of the 'eighties with the Japanese giants squaring up for a showdown as they plug every gap in the market place with a bewildering range of new and ever more sophisticated motor cycles.

Spoilt for Choice

Honda certainly started something when they introduced the first true mass-production Superbike, the CB750, back in 1968. For the big bike market has flourished to such a degree that by the start of 1982 Honda themselves offered no less than seven different Superbike models.

Most impressive from the mechanical point of view is the CBX–B. This is powered by an incredible across-the-frame, double overhead camshaft, six-cylinder engine that whacks out 100hp – sufficient to propel this beautifully proportioned machine at speeds up to 140mph.

Features include four valves per cylinder, five-speed gearbox, clock and electric starter while the latest B series machine has the moto cross developed Pro-link single-shock rear suspension, a fairing as standard and, along with Kawasaki's formidable Z1300, must rank as the ultimate sports-touring machine.

For the out-and-out touring rider, the man who likes to cover hundreds of miles a day at a more leisurely pace and who does not like to play at racers, Honda have two versions of the Gold Wing – the standard GL1100K–B and the lavishly

Honda's best selling CB750 range includes this F2 model with sports fairing

The Kawasaki Z1100GP in action. This fully equipped sports roadster is capable of speeds up to 140mph – twice the legal limit on British roads!

A Superbike for the super-tourer – the Honda GL1100B Gold Wing with water-cooled, flat four engine and shaft drive

equipped GL1100DX–B.

Completely different from anything they had previously built, the Gold Wing was launched in 1974 and it retains basically the same engine: a water-cooled, flat four with single overhead camshaft valve operation and a five-speed gear-box – an engine in fact very similar to the Alfa Sud car unit.

Originally this was of 999cc but the latest version has been bumped up to 1085cc and produces 85bhp. The engine is mounted in a massive frame with shaft drive and an unusual feature is that the fuel is carried in a tank under the seat – the normal 'tank' being a dummy which conceals the petrol and water filler caps, storage space, tool kit and fuses.

The standard model weighs in at 588lb while fairing, panniers and other extras push the de luxe version up to 627lb, the heaviest model in the Honda range.

At the opposite end of the motor cycling spectrum Honda catalogue the CB1100R – ostensibly a sports roadster but in reality built in strictly limited numbers and sold to riders who want to succeed in production events where the bikes must be raced in standard trim.

The engine is a replica of the 1062cc four-cylinder unit developed by Honda for Formula One and endurance events. This is an orthodox air-cooled, across the frame, double overhead camshaft unit with five-speed gearbox and chain final drive. The latest batch of engines give over 120hp and have a top speed of over 140mph – no wonder they do so well in races around the world!

These handbuilt machines are the most expensive Hondas on the market with a price tag of over £4000 but then they do come virtually ready to race with frontal fairing and single seat.

For the rider who prefers a slightly less highly tuned four-cylinder machine, Honda offer a choice of two – the CB900F–B and CB900F2–B, the latter complete with fairing. These two models, together with the CB750F, are the direct descendants of the CB750 of 1968, the bike that really started the Superbike craze.

Both 900cc and 750cc units are basically the same with four-cylinders, double overhead camshafts, four valves per cylinder and five-speed transmission. The bigger engines give 95hp, the smaller just a shade under 80 – the sort of power that the works racing machines of just a few years ago were striving to achieve!

Not content with across-the-frame six- and four-cylinder layouts supplemented by a flat, horizontally opposed four, Honda are to produce yet another completely new Superbike in 1982 – the VF750. This is powered by a a water-cooled, vee-four with four valves per cylinder, double overhead camshafts, an 'over-square' bore and stroke of 70×48.6mm with six-speed transmission and shaft drive.

Initially two models will be on sale. The VF750C with custom styling and 75bhp engine and a more sporting version with European styling and slightly hotter 78bhp engine which peaks at 9500rpm; the VF750S.

That is the Honda line up for the early 'eighties – four completely different engines, one of which is offered in three different capacity sizes, to give six different models – and they in turn are often

Top model in the Honda range – the CB1100R, a 140mph sports roadster

Opposite *Still going strong the* CB750F *is one of the latest models that started with the* CB750 *back in 1968*

Solid power. The Z1300 *with massive 120 horse power six-cylinder engine is the flagship of the Kawasaki line*

offered in custom, touring or sports versions . . . a dazzling choice.

Kawasaki were the first of the Japanese big four to respond to Honda's decision to enter the big-bike market. They are said to have had a large capacity four-cylinder machine under development when Honda launched the CB750 in 1968 but then held up further work until they had seen whether or not Superbikes would catch on. They did . . . and Kawasaki launched their Z900 three years later. This double overhead camshaft, four-cylinder, four-stroke with five-speed gearbox effectively stole the limelight from Honda and ruled the roost as the top-selling super sports model for a number of years.

That was in the days when Superbikes were few and when new model launches attracted a lot of attention. Now Kawasaki, like Honda, list four capacities in their Superbike range from 750cc to 1300cc and these split into two families – the air-cooled, four-cylinder engines and the water-cooled six.

Let's take a look at the biggest machine first. When the race between the factories to build the biggest, fastest and most impressive Superbike was at its height at the end of the 'seventies

Kawasaki decided to build the flagship to end all the arguments – and the result is the Z1300, a mighty machine powered by an across-the-frame, in-line, water-cooled, double overhead camshaft engine that would not disgrace a sports car!

Power from this impressive 1300cc unit is close to 120bhp with the delightfully smooth engine revving freely to over 8000. Transmission is by five-speed gearbox and shaft drive with the machine, ready for the road, weighing in at a massive 661lb. Trouble is that this sort of sophistication costs a lot of money – around £3250 on the UK market, slightly less than Honda's comparable CBX–B.

The Z1300 is a luxury tourer, fast and effortless. For the rider who goes more for the sporting image and likes a bit of snarl about his bike Kawasaki offer the Z1100GP, considered by many to be the equal of any sports roadster on the market.

Cast in the classic four-cylinder, across-the-frame mould popularised by the Italian Gilera and MV Agusta racers of the immediate post-war years, the Z1100GP is the latest and fastest in the line that started with the Z900 a decade ago.

Smooth power from Kawasaki – the six-cylinder Z1300 makes light of long distances

Power of the 1089cc (72.5 × 66mm bore and stroke) unit is 108bhp and to improve acceleration and fuel economy fuel injection is fitted, following the successful introduction of this system on Kawasaki's Z1000H, the first production motor cycle in the world to be so equipped.

As with many of today's Superbikes air is the main suspension medium, with air-adjustable forks up front and five load-position air shocks at the rear. If you do not want, or cannot afford, a ready-to-go production racer then Kawasaki have the Z1000J powered by a 998cc/102bhp version of their four-cylinder engine – or if you prefer a touring or custom model Kawasaki also have them in their Superbike range: the Z1100A is a 100bhp four with shaft drive while the Z1000LTD is a chopper version with that laid-back look preferred by some. Special features include a smaller rear wheel, stepped dual seat, high swept-back handlebars and a shorter exhaust system.

American styling has spread to Europe in recent years. This is the Kawasaki Z1000LTD with long fork, small tank, stepped seat and high 'bars

Just one of Kawasaki's family of robust four-cylinder Superbikes – the Z1100A

Japanese Battle

Caught on the hop by the incredible Superbike boom the other two factories of the Japanese big four, Suzuki and Yamaha, spent much of the 'seventies developing their big machines to match the Honda and Kawasaki models.

Suzuki's first effort was a water-cooled, three cylinder, two-stroke which was quiet, very fast and earned the nickname 'whispering death' because the handling was not, in the opinion of some, man enough to cope with the high top speed. Like the even fiercer H2R 750cc three-cylinder Kawasaki, on which one American test rider was able to do 200-yard wheelies (changing gear with the front wheel high in the air) it was killed off by the stringent air-pollution regulations which became law in California during the 'seventies – two-stroke engines could not, at that time, satisfy the emission laws.

While Barry Sheene was racing a modified 750cc Suzuki to many victories in the early and mid 'seventies the factory in Japan was designing a completely new range of four-strokes to replace

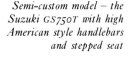

Semi-custom model – the Suzuki GS750T with high American style handlebars and stepped seat

the big two-strokes, knocked out of the American market by the new laws.

They succeeded brilliantly for when they launched the GS1000 in 1978 it was hailed by the Press as the best all-round Superbike on the market, fast, effortless, controllable and, above all, still light and compact by big-bike standards.

Now for the 'eighties Suzuki offer seven 750cc and over models. Top of the range are the two GSX1100's – the SZ with the ultra-modern Katana styling and the ET, the original model with more conventional lines. Both are powered by the same 1075cc four-cylinder, double overhead camshaft engine (with four valves per cylinder) but the Katana unit gives slightly more power: 104bhp compared to the 100 of the ET.

Following their original concept Suzuki have managed to keep the weight and bulk of their Superbikes down and the new Katana (Japanese for those long curved swords made famous by war films) tips the scales at a very creditable 510lb. Equipment includes air suspension, electric starter, double-disc front brakes with single-disc at the rear, light alloy rear swinging fork, racing-type anti-dive front forks and a small fairing with windscreen and mirrors.

New from Suzuki, the aggressively styled GSX1100 Katana

*Eye catching sports
roadster – the Suzuki
GSX1100*

Priced at under £3000 the biggest of the Katana range, styled in Germany by a small design studio, has proved a good seller since it was introduced in 1981 and is supplemented by a second Katana model, the GSX1000S. With an engine capacity of 997cc this 16-valve model is suitable for high-speed road work or the 1000cc class of production machine racing – or simply posing around town!

Two conventional models complete the Suzuki 1000cc Superbike range – the GS1000GT, a tourer with shaft drive, and the GS1000ET the latest version of the original sports GS1000 with the 997cc engine now uprated to give 90bhp and still reckoned to be one of the very best big bikes and, at around the £2000 mark, outstanding value for money.

Next model down the range is the GS850GT. This is another shaft-drive model and the transmission on these Suzukis is so good that although they are inevitably heavier than the chain-drive models they lose out very little when it comes to

top speed (the good old-fashioned chain is remarkably efficient in engineering terms) and gain a great deal in terms of lack of messy maintenance and the fact that the shaft will last the lifetime of the bike and not need replacing every few thousand miles. Certainly a buyer, unless he wants actually to race the machine, should always go for shaft drive.

Smallest of Suzuki's true Superbikes is the GSX750ET with sports 16-valve, 80hp engine and lavish standard equipment – a good buy for the person who wants a nimble, sports roadster.

Late on the Superbike scene, Yamaha got away to an uninspiring start with their first efforts – the XS750 three-cylinder, double overhead camshaft five-speeder and the XS1100 four. The XS750 proved a reliable tourer but little more while the bigger machine was so massive and heavy that it proved a slow seller.

Both remain in the range for the 'eighties, though in modified pepped-up form, but they are supplemented by two vee-twins and an enlarged

Equipped with shaft drive for the touring rider – the Suzuki GS1000GT

Black beauty – Yamaha's top of the range sports model, the XS1100S

825cc version of the triple.

Top of the range is the XS1100S, a sports version of the original XS1100 with the power increased to 95bhp. With an all-black finish this is an impressive bike and with a lower riding position, small handlebar fairing and shaft drive it is well worth considering by the serious, long-distance, touring rider.

Next in line is Japan's first big vee-twin, the TR1. The 981cc overhead camshaft engine produces a leisurely 70bhp to give this machine that lazy, mile-eating gait that is the trade mark of the big-twin. Special features include Yamaha's mono-shock rear suspension perfected on their road racers, a spine frame and a totally enclosed rear chain which should have a very much longer life than those left out in the open.

Competitively priced, the vee-twin Yamaha is also offered as a 750cc (XV750SE) but this model is sold only as a custom-chopper with longer forks, stepped dual seat, smaller rear wheel and modified exhaust. Curiously it does have one

The TR1, Yamaha's biggest vee-twin, has a capacity of 981cc and a top speed of 120mph

advantage over its bigger brother – it has shaft drive instead of chain.

The original three-cylinder 750cc model continues in the range as the XS750S but oddly enough the S does not mean (as it does on the XS1100S) sport – or if it does it is a misnomer – for this machine is another custom-chopper aimed more at the American market than at Europe.

Seventh and newest of the Yamaha Superbikes – and one which at last gives them a real challenger in the market – is the XJ750. This is an enlarged version of the XJ550 and XJ650 models that set new standards among mid-range bikes for styling, performance and economy.

The engine follows the path trodden by all three of their Japanese rivals, a double overhead camshaft across-the-frame four. But Yamaha have made this unit very narrow by taking the alternator off the end of the crankshaft, where it is usually the first thing to ground during vigourous cornering, and putting it behind the cylinders where it is driven by a counter-shaft.

With bore and stroke of 65×56.4mm the engine develops 81bhp at 9000rpm with a wide range of power and maximum torque (pulling power) at 7500rpm. Gearbox is a five-speeder and ignition is a transistor system without points. Weight has been kept down to 482lb – nearly 30lb less than the similar Honda model.

Among the space-age features of the Yamaha XJ750 is a computerised monitoring system with LCD display on the instrument panel that keeps an automatic eye on eight vital functions and gives an instant read-out of failures. For example, if a tail light bulb blows the rider will be informed of this by the word 'Tail' lighting up – and this will stay on until the fault is rectified.

Yamaha have paid great attention to the front fork, and the lessons learned from their programme of grand prix racing with American

Long range tourer – the Yamaha XV750SE vee-twin comes complete with transatlantic styling and shaft drive

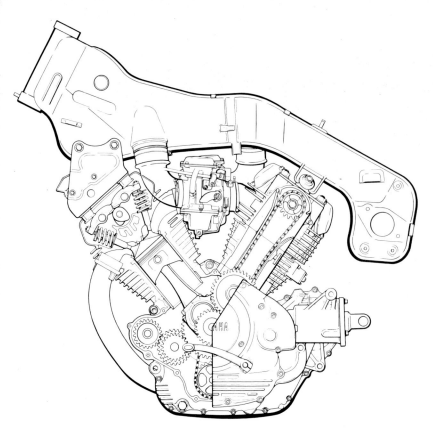

Cut-away drawing shows the layout of Yamaha's XV750SE vee-twin. Note the twin carburettors nestling in the vee of the cylinders

Top of the range models from Yamaha; the XS850, XS1100 and X1100S

Kenny Roberts and England's Barry Sheene are incorporated into the design of the xj750, which has an air-assisted fork with hydraulic anti-dive mechanism built in. This prevents the front end dipping when the big twin-disc front brakes are applied hard at speed.

Yes, the battle between the Japanese makers for the lucrative Superbike market is well and truly on and the trend started by Honda with the cb750 back in 1968 has grown to near flood proportions with the big four offering close to 30 different 750cc-and-over models ranging from vee-twin, straight-three and four-cylinder models to vee-fours and air- and water-cooled straight sixes . . . certainly a far cry from the days of the 'fifties when the British vertical twins ruled the roost.

European Challengers

The BSA–Triumph group was the first to be knocked out by the flood of Japanese Superbikes. Norton followed but other European factories have managed to keep going – notably BMW of Germany and Benelli, Ducati, Moto Guzzi and Laverda of Italy – while a new factory, at Daventry in England is to produce the Hesketh the first new British Superbike for over a decade.

Firm favourites with serious long-distance riders around the world, BMW now make a range of five over-750cc big bikes – all powered by their traditional air-cooled, horizontally opposed, flat twin with the engine mounted across the frame so that the finned cylinders stick out both sides. Valve operation is by push rods and transmission by five-speed gearboxes to a shaft drive; so long the hallmark of BMW but now copied very successfully by the Japanese.

Charm of the big BMWs lies in their ability to eat up the miles in a relaxed way – the twin-

Fast, long distance journeys are a joy on the BMW R100RS

The author took this shot of a BMW R80GS he was testing high in the Atlas Mountains in Morocco

in Spandau, West Berlin, having moved from the traditional home in Munich). It too has a fairing as standard but this is less racy and allows a more upright riding position.

Completing the BMWs powered by the big 980cc engine are the R100CS, a sports model without the refinements of the RS, and the R100, the basic model with detuned engine (66bhp).

Getting away from their slightly old-fashioned road rider image the German factory launched their first trail bike – and the first trail Superbike in the world – the R80GS in 1980. With long travel front fork, the rear wheel supported on only one side (by the beefed-up shaft drive), white finish and red seat the R80GS is visually very different from any other BMW.

But the way it goes and handles soon made it a firm favourite and it is now one of the factory's best sellers. Although designed for occasional off-road use it is an ideal commuter bike, equally at home on 70mph motorway and weaving in and out of traffic jams where the wide bars and upright riding position make it easy to control. Weight has been kept down to a reasonable 368lb and, like all BMWs, the R80GS is economical, averaging well over 40 to the gallon.

Benelli were actually the first to produce a six-cylinder Superbike, a 750cc, in the early 'seventies though it did not go into volume production for several years. It remains in production though with the capacity increased to 903cc to combat the bigger and faster six-cylinder Honda/Kawasaki designs.

A noisy, out-and-out sports machine the Benelli handles well and has a top speed of over 120mph but is tiring to ride and lacks the sophistication of the latest Japanese models. Unusual feature is a double rear chain (like two normal chains side-by-side) which prolongs chain life – but costs a small fortune to replace when it wears out.

The two Ducati Superbikes, the 900ss and the Darmah Sport, have built up a wide following around the world and usually win racing events for twin-cylinder sports machines – and often

cylinder engines virtually ticking over at 5000rpm while the tarmac reels away under the wheels at over 100mph.

Top of the range is the impressive R100RS. This is a sports tourer that comes complete with race-style, wind-tunnel tested fairing, quartz clock, rev counter and first-aid kit. The 980cc engine (94 × 70.6mm) produces 70hp at 7000rpm to give the machine a top speed of 120mph – and a cruising speed very little lower. The excellent fairing really does protect the rider from the buffeting air and allows him to concentrate on his riding and not just on hanging on, often the case when riding an unstreamlined machine at speed for any distance.

Powered by the same engine the R100RT is the top touring model from BMW (the factory is now ones open to four cylinders as well.

For these unusual vee-twins with their engines mounted so that one cylinder sticks forward near horizontally while the other is inclined slightly backward, handle extremely well and produce usable power over a wide rev range.

Alone among sports motor cycles the 900ss has desmodromic valves – closed as well as opened by cams and without conventional valve springs. Power is a relatively lowly 68bhp but coupled to the handling and low weight of 415lb it makes the 900ss a formidable rival and a machine that road testers around the world enthuse over. Definitely a bike for the connoisseur. The Darmah Sport is fitted with a detuned engine of the same capacity (864cc, 60bhp).

The famous old Moto Guzzi factory at Mandello del Lario in Italy's northern lake district offers a range of four vee-twin Superbikes, but these are very different from the Ducatis. The engines are mounted across the frame so that the cylinders stick out on each side. Drive is via a five-speed gearbox and shaft and it is interesting to note that the unusual engine is one developed from a unit first designed to power a small all-terrain army four-wheeler, a sort of mini Jeep.

Fastest model in the range, at an impressive 130mph, is the 844cc Le Mans. Long, low and lean, this Moto Guzzi looks just what it is – a super sports roadster that handles and goes extremely well. The engine produces 78bhp and this coupled to a bike that weighs only 435lb makes for a first-class road-going Superbike.

Unusual feature of the Moto Guzzis is the coupled braking system. The foot pedal, which normally only works the rear brake on a motor cycle, is also coupled to one of the two front disc brakes. This means that a rider operating the rear brake automatically gets half braking power on the front wheel with the normal handlebar lever working the second front disc.

Two other Moto Guzzi models are powered by

Another Italian beauty – the 850cc vee-twin Moto Guzzi Le Mans

basically the same 844cc engine: the 850T4 and the 850T3 California. The 850T4 is a European touring version of the Le Mans with a detuned engine while the California, as the name implies, is made specifically for the American market and comes complete with sit-up-and-beg riding position, footboards, windscreen and panniers.

Fourth model in the range has a bigger engine with capacity enlarged to 949cc but the power kept down to 70bhp. The result is a unit with a lot of flexible power which makes it ideal for the SP1000NT, a luxury touring machine.

Laverda have based their popularity squarely on producing super sports models with gut-wrenching performance and three 1116cc models, powered by basically the same three-

cylinder, double overhead camshaft engine, head their range.

Top model is the 1200 Formula Mirage, a street legal racer capable of speeds over 140mph. The most expensive Italian machine on the market, the Mirage comes complete with just about the best equipment that money can buy, including Brembo disc brakes and alloy Astralite wheels.

For the long-distance man Laverda offer the 1200TTS Mirage with detuned engine and handlebar and engine/leg fairing as standard while the basic 1200 completes the big-bike range. Powered by a 981cc version of the same engine the Jota is the fourth Laverda Superbike and still just about the most popular with a racing riding

position and a top speed of around 130mph.

While the Japanese plug every gap in the Superbike market and the Germans and Italians try to hang on, the British Hesketh concern has taken the bold step of actually coming into the market. Headed by Lord Alexander Hesketh, the man who sponsored Formula One car world champion James Hunt during his early years on four-wheels, they are to launch a lusty, mainly British 1000cc vee-twin on the market during 1982.

The double overhead camshaft, 86bhp engine, a modified version of an original British Weslake design, is mounted Ducati-style to give a small frontal area, low centre of gravity and excellent balance.

Hesketh are aiming at the top end of the market; for the man who wants an exclusive modern-day classic motor cycle and the price of close to £5000 reflects this – over twice the cost of the Yamaha TR1 1000cc vee-twin.

New challenger from England – the Hesketh V1000 went into production early in 1982 with a near £5000 price tag

Even so the Hesketh is not as expensive as Harley-Davidson's top offering, the extraordinary FLT–1340 Tour-Glide which weighs in at a massive 725lb and whose 1340cc vee-twin engine produces 70bhp.

Harleys are of course made in America, the only surviving factory of what was once a thriving industry (just as Triumph are the only surviving British factory from an even larger number of British manufacturers). They survive because enough American riders like them and will ride nothing else, but compared to Japanese and European machines they are under-powered, over-weight and over-priced.

The New Wave

Throughout the 'seventies the Japanese factories vied with each other to produce the biggest, fastest and most prestigious Superbikes – often seemingly ignoring what the potential buyer actually wanted!

The culmination of this power struggle was the six-cylinder 1000cc Honda CBX and the mammoth water-cooled, six-cylinder Kawasaki Z1300. Both machines produced well over 100hp, both cost a lot of money and would obviously sell only in small numbers – but then they are flagships to be proudly displayed at exhibitions around the world to prove just what their makers can do when given the chance.

The authorities were not impressed. Japan already had a 750cc capacity maximum and West Germany introduced a 100hp top limit in an effort to stem what they saw as a dangerous development. In any case the Japanese themselves realised that they had reached the limit and that in future it would be better to concentrate on developing their mid-range models because these are the ones that sell in vast numbers – and this had led to the new wave of mini Superbikes now reaching the market.

The 500 to 600cc bracket has always been a popular one in Europe. In fact in the 'thirties and 'forties the top sports models from the then dominating British industry was virtually always a 500 – the legendary Norton International, Rudge Ulster, Ariel Red Hunter and BSA Gold Star; all powered by 500cc engines and all capable of over 90mph.

By today's standards their power output was puny – around the 40bhp mark was the most skilful tuners could extract. But they were considered big enough and powerful enough for the often tricky and treacherous road conditions of the day.

As roads improved and motorways became popular so speeds went up, but for the great majority of riders a modern-day mini Superbike will do all that he requires – and will do it far cheaper than one of full-sized Superbikes.

Kawasaki were perhaps the first to realise this when they produced a range of light, tractable double overhead camshaft fours in the late 'seventies – starting with a 650cc and soon followed by a 500cc.

Now they list five models in this money-earning segment of the market. Priced at half the cost of the Z1300 the Z650F2 is the top model and boasts all the modern technological goodies – air forks, adjustable rear dampers, electric starter, cast alloy wheels, headlamp flasher – the lot.

It is supplemented by a custom model with American styling, including longer forks, high 'bars, stepped seat and a smaller 16-in rear wheel with fatter tyre. Selling at the same price as the two bigger-engined models is the Z550GP, the super sports model in the three-machine 550cc range. Like the other two it has a top speed of close to 120mph and comes complete with a small streamlining, oil-cooler and rev-counter. A custom version, the Z550LTD, and a roadster, the Z550A2 complete the range of Kawasaki mini Superbikes – and, in these days of rocketing fuel prices, it is worth noting that all better 50mpg and, ridden touring style, can get over 60 miles from a gallon.

One of the first of the new wave of mini Superbikes – the Kawasaki Z550GP

Suzuki were also early in the field with attractive mid-range models. Now, like Kawasaki, they list five with the Katana-styled GS650GX the top-priced model at around £1700 – more than £1000 cheaper than the top of the Superbike range GSX1100SZ.

Unusually the actual engine size is bigger than the model number – 673cc (62 × 55.8mm bore and stroke) – and produces a creditable 73hp which, coupled to a weight of 480lb, gives a top speed of around the 120mph mark. Another plus is the fact that this smallest model in the Katana range has shaft drive – a curious omission from the larger models because having bigger and more powerful engines they impose heavier loadings on the final-drive chain.

Sharing the same basic engine, though in a less highly tuned state, is the GS650GTX, the orthodox-styled stablemate for the Katana. Three 549cc models complete the list: the GS550M, smallest of the Katana range, the highly rated GS550EX, an orthodox sportster and the now almost obligatory American-styled custom-chopper. Like the 550cc Kawasakis, the three smaller Suzuki have six-speed gearboxes compared to the five-speeders of the bigger machines.

After a slow start Yamaha has obviously sensed the enormous potential of the mid-range machines and during 1981 produced two of the best, the XJ550 and XJ650. Powered by new, slim and very powerful four-cylinder double overhead camshaft engines with six-speed gearboxes, these XJ models really are mini Superbikes in every sense of the word: fast, economical, reasonably priced and with superb handling which means that on anything but flat-out speed they compete on equal terms with the bigger machines.

Not satisfied with those two models Yamaha launched a completely new 550cc sports machine at the Paris Show late in 1981. Code-named the XZ550, this is powered by a water-cooled, vee-twin but, unlike the Honda CX500, the Yamaha engine is mounted fore-and-aft to give a very slim frontal area.

An impressive newcomer to the mid-range is the Yamaha XZ550, powered by a 64 horse power double overhead camshaft vee-twin

Yamaha's all new XZ550 is powered by a slim vee-twin that fits inside the frame tubes. Note the shaft drive and cantilever rear suspension

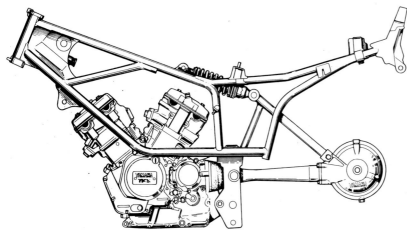

Normally vee-twins are lazy, slow-revving engines designed more for touring than sports use. Not so the Yamaha xz550. For the engine, with double overhead camshafts and four valves per cylinder, spins to 9500rpm and whacks out 64bhp – equal to 116bhp per litre which is good by any standard.

Air-forks are fitted and rear suspension is by Yamaha's monoshock system where the whole of the rigidly braced rear fork pivots and is controlled by a single unit tucked away out of sight below seat and tank. This model really is a breakthrough and it will be interesting to trace its progress through the 'eighties.

Strangely Honda, the biggest of the Japanese big four, seem to have been left a little behind in this new market. Their water-cooled, vee-twin cx500 with transverse engine and shaft-drive is now dated, which leaves the cb650z as their only real challenger. This is very much an updated version of earlier models and Honda are certain to introduce new models in the 550–650 bracket very soon.

Of the European factories both bmw and Ducati have introduced new machines in this category during the last two years. The bmw r65 is a first-class sports roadster with a 50bhp version of the traditional bmw flat-twin engine, easy and comfortable to ride.

The Ducati 600 Pantah is an enlarged version

Biggest of the new range of four-cylinder Yamahas – the XJ750. The 650cc and 550cc versions are near identical

A top mid-capacity sports model, the 600cc Ducati Pantah combines usable power with fine handling

European mid-range challenger, the 500cc Moto Guzzi Monza

of the original 500cc model, powered by a really modern engine with belt-driven single overhead camshafts. Light yet powerful and with the usual superb Ducati road holding, it has proved a winner in production machine events – to the surprise and chagrin of the Japanese factories – including the Formula Two race at the Isle of Man TT.

The Laverda Montjuic and Moto Guzzi V50 Monza also rate a mention. The Montjuic is a street legal production racer which costs more than many 1000cc bikes but goes, handles and stops like a racer. Power unit is a 497cc vertical twin with double overhead camshafts which produces over 50bhp to give a top speed of 115mph.

Moto Guzzi's offering is far less rorty; a really compact little 500cc air-cooled-vee-twin with shaft drive and top speed of just over the ton – a thoroughly practical motor cycle.

Turbo Power

In the history of road-going motor cycles 1982 is certain to go down as the year of the turbo-charger. For all four of the Japanese factories and at least one European maker have announced they are to sell turbo models, with Honda actually winning the battle to be the first to get their machine into the dealers' showrooms.

The virtue of turbo-charging is that it uses the normally wasted flow of exhaust gases to spin a small impellor turbine which in turn pressurises and speeds the flow of air and petrol into the engine.

This means that for a given capacity the technician can get more power out of a turbo-charged engine than from a normally aspirated one. In Formula One car racing, where Renault and Ferrari have pioneered the turbo, engines of this type can be only half the cubic capacity of normally aspirated units – 1500cc compared to 3000cc. However, on smaller engines the turbo is likely to be less efficient and the Federation Internationale Motocycliste (FIM), governing body of motor cycle sport, are to give turbos a 40 per cent handicap for racing (turbo-charged engines up to 600cc competing against normally aspirated 1000cc engines).

It is worthwhile noting here that bikes lag behind cars in turbo development for two main reasons. Firstly because turbos do not work on the extremely high-powered two-stroke engines that dominate two-wheeled grand prix racing. Secondly because, compared to production-car engines, those fitted to sports motor cycles are extremely efficient. In other words until the 'eighties motor cycle designers got the extra power they wanted by building bigger and more efficient normally aspirated engines.

Not so in the car world. There manufacturers saw a relatively inexpensive way of boosting the power of existing engines and a rash of turbos hit the market. Backed by publicity they caught the imagination of a sector of the public who thought the turbo provided something for nothing.

The problem is that because the turbo is spun by the exhaust gases it only really works when the engine is revving. At low engine speeds those gases simply are not moving fast enough to give the necessary boost. Moreover, at high revs the boost pressure is too strong and the system has to incorporate a safety valve; called a waste-gate in turbo parlance.

Because of these inherent faults the turbo poses two problems to the motor cyclist. Firstly the real power of the engine is likely to come in with a bang when the turbo starts to work just as the engine is getting into its normal power band.

Secondly there is likely to be a slight time lag between closing the throttle and the engine slowing. This is because it takes time for the turbo, which spins at incredible speeds (up to 180,000rpm) to slow down – and all the while it is spinning it is trying to pump fresh fuel into the engine.

These problems, along with others (such as how adequately to lubricate the high-revving turbo in the event of a sudden engine stop – for example if the rider stalls the engine while attempting a grand prix start at the traffic lights) are now being tackled but the cost of overcoming them is such that the first turbo to go on the

The first turbo-charged production motor cycle – the Honda CX500 Turbo, launched after five years of development

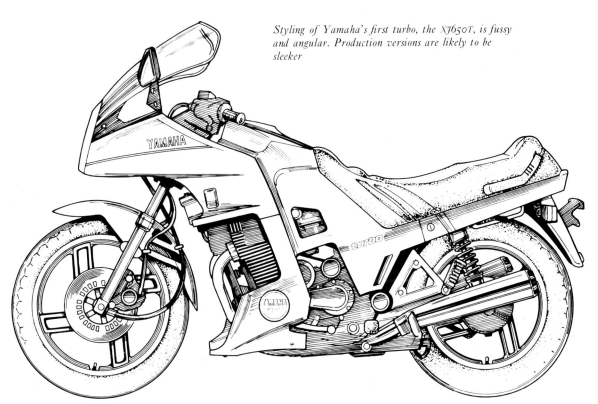

Styling of Yamaha's first turbo, the XJ650T, is fussy and angular. Production versions are likely to be sleeker

market, the Honda CX500 Turbo is to cost over twice the price of a standard CX500!

Exhibited at a number of international shows the CX500 Turbo was officially launched at the Paris Show in October 1981. Honda claim they have chosen to turbo-charge the CX500 because they feel that the vee-twin engine is one of the most difficult to turbo-charge – and that if they can succeed then tackling four-cylinder engines will be easy!

The logic of this argument is hard to grasp. The potential turbo-buyer is someone impressed by power, performance and, above all, looks. And to turbo-charge the basically rather mundane touring CX500 is rather like trying to turn the proverbial sow's ear into a silk purse.

Having said that there is no doubt that the Honda CX500 Turbo is an attractive motor cycle with integral fairing, cleverly styled seat and tank,

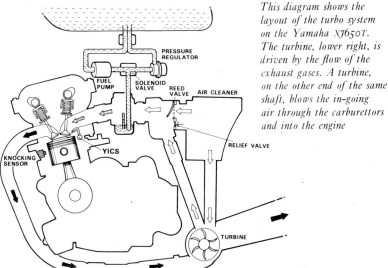

This diagram shows the layout of the turbo system on the Yamaha XJ650T. The turbine, lower right, is driven by the flow of the exhaust gases. A turbine, on the other end of the same shaft, blows the in-going air through the carburettors and into the engine

Yamaha launched their first turbo – the XJ650T – at the Paris Show at the end of 1981

eye-catching silver, grey and red colour scheme and with 'Turbo' in huge letters along the silencers on each side of the machine – no good spending all that extra money if no one knows about it!

Power of the water-cooled, overhead camshaft, 500cc, across-the-frame, vee-twin CX500 engine is boosted from a healthy 50hp to a claimed 76 at 8000rpm while Honda have done well to keep the weight down to about 490lb, only ten up on the standard model.

But the fuel injection/turbo-charging is incredibly complicated and a mini computer is housed in the tail of the machine. Its task, according to the Honda handout is to . . . 'ensure that each cylinder gets exactly the right amount of fuel it needs under any normal circumstance; it also has to act safely under any normal one. It does this by taking readings of the throttle opening, atmospheric temperature and pressure, engine coolant temperature and individual cylinder intake pressure, then compares these with its twin programmes. The integrated answer results in each solenoid-controlled injector opening just long enough to admit the exact amount of fuel required. . . .' No comment!

If you are a person who loves modern technology, is impressed by the latest craze and must have the latest then the Honda CX500 Turbo is for you, but I cannot help feeling that there are easier, simpler and cheaper ways of producing a 76hp motor cycle.

Yamaha followed Honda along the turbo trail and they too had their first production effort, the XJ650T at the Paris Show. Unlike Honda they chose an already highly desirable mid-range sports model, the XJ650, and added a turbo.

They had earlier dabbled with a turbo-charged XS1100 but, as they rightly say, that is a power unit that hardly needed a turbo! So development was concentrated on the XJ650 and Yamaha decided on a very much simpler turbo system than Honda.

Normal carburettors are retained. Yamaha saying . . . 'this is a cost-saving measure over the obviously expensive computer-controlled fuel injection and in practical applications the carburettor is perfectly adequate . . .' an obvious snipe at Honda!

The Yamaha system boosts the power from 73 to 85bhp but the styling of the model shown at Paris was angular with none of the flair and grace of the normal XJ range.

Unlike Honda and Yamaha, who have both gone for turbo models fitted with fairings, Kawasaki have announced an out-and-out sports turbo, though this is unlikely to be on sale until 1983. Based on the four-cylinder Z750 and with the turbo-charger mounted low down in front of the crankcase, Kawasaki claim 100hp for this

Not to be outdone by their rivals, Kawasaki issued this picture of their first turbo, the Z750T, at the end of 1981. They claim a power output of 100bhp

Turbo of the future? The prototype BMW Futuro twin is fitted with a turbo-charged, flat twin engine

aggressively styled model.

Suzuki, last of the Japanese big four to admit to developing turbo models, launched their prototype, a four-cylinder 650, at the Tokyo Show late in 1981 while in Europe the little Morini factory are experimenting with a turbo-charged version of their 500cc vee-twin.

Will the turbo catch on or is it just a sales gimmick? That is a question that is likely to keep motor cyclists talking for several years as the turbo war hots up. It will be interesting to see which way it goes.

Four-Strokes Supreme

While two-strokes dominate grand prix racing the big four-strokes reign supreme in long-distance endurance events: races like the French 24-hour Bol d'Or and the Spanish 24-hours of Montjuich where four-stroke stamina outlasts two-stroke speed.

All the bikes raced in this class are modified Superbikes powered by basically the same engine as the man in the street can buy. And to encourage four-stroke racing the Federation Internationale Motocycliste instigated the Formula One class (open to 1000cc four-strokes and 600cc two-strokes) for modified catalogue sports bikes.

Both classes have been well supported by the manufacturers who realise the important publicity to be gained from international racing successes and in addition to the World Championship endurance series, with rounds in most major motor cycling countries, Formula One events are held at the Isle of Man TT and as part of the famous March speed week at Daytona that culminates in the Daytona 200.

Endurance honours in 1981 were shared by Kawasaki and Honda, with Kawasaki taking the endurance world title while Honda came out tops in the Bol d'Or, far and away the most important endurance race in the world and annually watched by crowds of up to 70,000 race-mad Frenchman.

The Kawasaki endurance effort was masterminded by their French importer Xavier Maugendre who had been striving to win the championship, without success, for several years. He entered two factory-built but French pre-

One of the Kawasaki endurance team prepares for the start of the Bol d'Or, and 24 hours of flat-out riding

Honda power. American Freddie Spencer cranks his works 997cc four-cylinder Honda endurance racer to the limit

pared machines and, despite Honda opposition, finished up with a resounding one-two placing in the final championship table.

Tuned to give close to 140hp and with weight cut to 380lb the Kawasakis had a top speed of over 150mph – but covered only 18 miles per gallon! Interesting features included the use of good old-fashioned carburettors though Kawasaki's top sports model, the Z1100GP, has

fuel injection and the fitting of only one rear suspension unit on the otherwise orthodox rear suspension fork.

For the Bol d'Or, in which engines up to 1300cc are allowed, Kawasaki used four-cylinder engines with the capacity enlarged to 1150cc but they ran into trouble and victory went to a factory 997cc Honda ridden by the French pairing of Dominique Sarron and Jean-Claude Jaubert.

The engine of the endurance Honda is in fact based on the latest version of the CB750 – so the bike that started it all is still very much with us! Peak revs are just over the 10,000 mark but for long-distance events the riders normally keep them down to 9500 in the interests of engine longevity.

It is interesting to note that during a 24-hour race a typical bike will use 120 gallons of petrol and will wear out three or four rear tyres, two front tyres plus several sets of brake pads – and the engine will complete over 13,000,000 revs!

Suzuki won the Bol d'Or in 1980 with a Yoshimura tuned GS1000 but were never in the running in 1981 though they did win the final round of the endurance series at Donington Park in late September. A technical point here is that despite the talked of superiority of four-valve per cylinder layouts, Yoshimura sticks to the GS two-valve head, claiming it gives better gas-flow.

Yamaha, up to now, have kept away from big four-stroke racing, preferring to concentrate their efforts on developing two-strokes for grand prix racing, though their French importer Sonauto did much to liven up the Bol d'Or for several years by entering a team of four-cylinder TZ750 two-stroke racers, specially modified for long-distance racing.

It is estimated the Sonauto spent £500,000 on this project over a three-year term but finally gave up after they again failed to win in 1980.

In British and American racing the Formula One class (called the Superbike class in the States but basically the same) has made great progress since it was introduced in the late 'seventies.

The big battle in English racing during 1981

Frenchman Jean-Claude Jaubert shared this 997cc factory Honda with compatriot Dominique Sarron to win the 1981 Bol d'Or 24-hour race

Opposite *Moriwaki-tuned Kawasakis challenged strongly for Superbike/Formula One honours throughout 1981*

Centre of attention – a factory Honda endurance racer before the start of the 24-hour Bol d'Or

was the struggle between New Zealander Graeme Crosby on a works Yoshimura Suzuki and England's Ron Haslam on a factory Honda. Crosby finished the year as the more successful by winning the Isle of Man TT and the Formula One championship decided over rounds at all the main British circuits.

Crosby also did well at Daytona where he finished a close second to his Yoshimura Suzuki team-mate Wes Cooley. However, despite this fine start to the season Suzuki lost the American

Superbike title to Eddie Lawson and Kawasaki.

In fact Formula One Production Machine racing has really caught on around the world because the basic machines are available, cost only a fraction of a grand prix replica machine and importers are prepared to support the class because the bikes raced are easily recognisable by the spectating public as being catalogue models that they can buy and ride – a far cry from today's specialised grand prix two-strokes.

Rules vary from country to country. In South

New Zealander Graeme Crosby (Suzuki) gives a victory salute after winning at Daytona. Opposite With the Suzuki on which he won the 1981 Isle of Man Classic TT

Africa the bikes must be stock with no engine mods but silencers can be removed and racing megaphones fitted. The theory being that noise adds to the excitement of the sport.

In Australia's most prestigious race, the Castrol Six Hour, the scrutineers insist all bikes must be absolutely stock. No modifications are allowed and one winning team was actually disqualified because they had added washers to the front suspension to give them a touch more cornering clearance!

In open-class racing Honda have struck a great blow for the big four-strokes by contesting the hard-fought British Superbike Championship.

VICTORY LANE
ELL SUPERBIKE "100"
DAYTONA, U.S.A.

In Daytona's Victory Lane after the 1981 Superbike race, Suzuki's Graeme Crosby and Wes Cooley celebrate their 1-2 ahead of Honda's Freddie Spencer

This is open to two-stroke grand prix racing machines and until 1981 had always been won by a two-stroke.

Honda decided to have a crack at the title in 1981 and entered their Formula One competitors Ron Haslam and Joey Dunlop on modified Formula One machines. These had the engines enlarged to 1123cc with the power upped to 144bhp. Even so they were heavier and bigger than the two-stroke TZ750 Yamahas and RG500 Suzukis that most of their rivals were riding and a hard battle ensued.

After racing in rounds at all the major British circuits Haslam won the title from South African Kork Ballington on a factory grand prix two-stroke Kawasaki. The big four-strokes had finally proved they can do it!

Straight Line Power

One type of competition in which big four-stroke engines have always been tops is drag racing – the straight-line sport made popular in the United States in which contestants pit themselves in pairs against the clock on a quarter-mile tarmac strip.

The clutch starts demand tremendous torque. The ability to produce power over a wide rev range is the key to success and the emergence of so many different large-capacity Superbikes has given the drag racers a whole range of suitable engines to choose from.

In the 'seventies the top men preferred to get power by adding engines. Culmination of this trend was American Russ Collins' machine which was powered by three 1200cc four-cylinder

Two of the fastest men in the world on the line at Santa Pod. Left is Sam Wills of America – in the background Henk Vink of Holland. Both are on supercharged Kawasakis

Best from Britain – Jeff Byne has run 8.02s with a terminal speed of 181mph on this twin-engined Triumph

Honda engines while his main challenger, Tom Christenson, raced a double-engined Norton with a total capacity of 1600cc. In England John Hobbs on a twin-engined Weslake (2×850cc) was the man to beat.

But these machines were very heavy and gradually the tide of development turned in favour of lighter, more manageable single-engined dragsters and despite their lack of total horse power they have beaten all records set by the brute-power multi-engined machines.

At the start of the 1982 season Bo O'Brochta from Florida was the quickest man in the world over the quarter mile with a time of 7.08 seconds and a terminal speed, measured over the final few yards of the run, of an incredible 197mph – mind boggling when you consider that this speed was achieved from a standing start at the end of a 440-

yard run, little over the length of four football pitches!

O'Brochta uses a single 1200cc Kawasaki four-cylinder engine. This is supercharged and, running on a special brew of fuel that contains close to 90 per cent of oxygen-bearing Nitro Methane, he claims a total output of 400hp. This sounds on the high side but his record is a powerful argument.

It is one thing to get the power – quite another to translate it into speed down the strip. Transmission is vital and O'Brochta uses a two-speed set up with a compressed-air system, activated by a trigger on the left handlebar, to shift from first to second as he hurtles down the tarmac. Secondary drive is by heavy-duty chain to a car-type rim fitted with a massive, flat treadless tyre which is warmed and softened to make it sticky before O'Brochta goes to the start.

Fastest man in Europe for several years, Dutchman Henk Vink was also Kawasaki-powered, but during 1981 he lost his crown to Sweden's Stefan Reisten who clocked 7.74 secs with a terminal speed of 193mph. His machine

200mph ahead! American Bo O'Brochta steadies his supercharged 1200cc Kawasaki on the line as he prepares for the getaway. His record time over the quarter mile is 7.08s with a terminal speed of nearly 197mph

Most successful European drag racer, Dutchman Henk Vink smokes away from the start on his Kawasaki powered machine

Pro Stock class dragsters are not allowed superchargers and have to use road tyres. This is Geoff Stilwell with his Z1-R1000cc Kawasaki

was powered by a Yamaha XS1100 four-cylinder, double overhead camshaft engine with the normal gearbox and shaft-drive removed and replaced by a two-speed transmission and chain similar to O'Brochta's.

In addition to the out-and-out record machines drag racing has a class for basically stock machines. Superchargers are banned, they must run on normal pump petrol, use the standard gearbox and transmission and while extensive frame and engine modifications are allowed, they must at least look like the originals.

Top Britain in this class as the sport went into 1982 was Brian Johnson on his immaculate Kawasaki-powered machine named Imperial Wizard. He beat the 9-sec barrier with a best time of 8.98 secs and a terminal speed of 151mph.

One thing is certain. All these records will soon be beaten, for with the motor cycle makers producing more and more Superbikes there is going to be no lack of suitable engines for the drag racers to use for years to come.

Top British Pro Stock competitor Brian Johnson on his Kawasaki 'Imperial Wizard'. Using road tyres and pump petrol he has recorded 8.98s/151mph

Immaculately prepared – Brian Johnson's Imperial Wizard Kawasaki topped the Pro Stock class in England in 1981

Index